UNUSUAL Histories

VELOCITY

The Curious, Captivating,

UNUSUAL
HISTORY OF
SPORTS

by Lucia Raatma

Consultant: Dr. Craig R. Coenen
Professor of History
Mercer County Community College

CAPSTONE PRESS
a capstone imprint

Velocity is published by Capstone Press,
1710 Roe Crest Drive, North Mankato, Minnesota 56003.
www.capstonepub.com

Books published by Capstone Press are manufactured with paper containing at least 10 percent post-consumer waste.

Library of Congress Cataloging-in-Publication Data
Raatma, Lucia.
The curious, captivating, unusual history of sports / by Lucia Raatma.
p. cm.—(Velocity. unusual histories)
Summary: "Describes the history of sports, featuring little-known facts and bizarre inside information"—Provided by publisher.
Includes bibliographical references and index.
ISBN 978-1-4296-7537-6 (library binding)
1. Sports—History—Juvenile literature. I. Title.
GV571.R33 2012
796.09—dc23   2011020704

Editorial Credits
Jennifer Besel, editor; Ashlee Suker, designer; Svetlana Zhurkin, media researcher;
    Laura Manthe, production specialist

Photo Credits: Comstock Klips, 21 (top right); Corbis, 14 (middle left), Bettmann, 32 (top), Neal Preston, 25 (top right), Underwood & Underwood, 14 (bottom); Dreamstime: Aleksandar Jocic, 16 (bottom), Lunamarina, 24 (back), Sarah Dusautoir, 9 (bottom), Zairbek Mansurov, 41 (top right); Getty Images: FPG, 18 (middle); iStockphoto: Duncan Walker, 16 (middle), Ron Brancato, 45 (middle left); Library of Congress, cover (bottom), 13 (top), 14 (middle right), 15 (top), 19 (top), 22 (top and bottom), 24 (middle), 30 (all), 31 (top left), 32 (bottom), 42 (middle left and right); Newscom: AFP/OPP/Don Emmert, 33 (top), AFP/Timothy A. Clary, 28, 31 (middle), akg-images, 7 (top), akg-images/Peter Connolly, 4 (bottom), Album/Universal Pictures/Alphaville Films, 40 (middle inset), Icon SMI/Anne Hiles, 39 (top left), Icon SMI/Aurelien Meunier, 39 (top right), Icon SMI/Ray Grabowski, 17 (bottom), Icon SMI/SportsAge, 13 (middle), KRT/Bob Coglianese, 34 (top), KRT/Julian H. Gonzalez, 8 (top), PHOTOlink/Mary Lupo, 41 (bottom), Popperfoto/KPA/United Archives, 9 (top), 15 (middle), SIPA/Regan, 35, TSN/Icon SMI, 31 (bottom), UP/Lori Shepler, 36 (top left), UPI Photo Service/Jason Szenes, 43 (middle right), ZUMA Press, 38 (right), ZUMA Press/KPA, 8 (bottom); Shutterstock: Alexander Kalina, 17 (top), Alexander Potapov, 44 (middle left), Anna Subbotina, 25 (top left), 29 (top right), 40 (top), Aspen Photo, 13 (bottom), 25 (bottom), Bill Florence, 12 (bottom), Brailescu Cristian, 45 (bottom right), Cindy Hughes (gym floor), cover (top), 36 (top right), cjmac, 39 (bottom left), cjpdesigns, 34 (bottom right), cozyta (track lanes), 1 (front), 7 (back), 48 (back), D. Silva, 36 (bottom), diless, 14–15 (back), donatas1205, 44–45 (back), Dusty Cline, 21 (bottom right), EuroPhotoGraphics, 5, Fel1ks, 8–9 (back), Francesco Abrignani, 6 (bottom), 44 (middle right), Gemenacom, 16 (top), grynold, 44 (top left and bottom right), Haslam Photography/Ben Haslam, 20 (bottom front), ifong, 43 (top right), imagelab, 45 (middle right), ingret, 21 (bottom left), jannoon028 (grass), cover (top), Jerry Sharp, 19 (middle), Jo Crebbin, 43 (middle left), Juha Sompinmäki, 7 (bottom), Kamira, 6 (top), kanate (grass field), 1 (back) and throughout, kots (rays), 4 (top) and throughout, Left Eyed Photography, 39 (top middle), LesPalenik, 26 (top), Lev Radin, 41 (top left), LittleRambo (frame), 14 (top), Marten Czamanske, 40 (bottom), Melica, 42 (middle right), Neale Cousland, 34 (bottom left), Nelson Marques, 26 (bottom), Ninell (books), 42 (top), olly, 42 (bottom), patrimonio designs limited, 45 (top left), Pete Saloutos, 29 (top left), Phil Anthony, 15 (bottom), photogolfer, 23 (top), 33 (bottom), 39 (bottom middle and right), Roman Gorielov, 23 (bottom), Ronald Sumners, 20 (middle), Rui Alexandre Araujo, 27, RusGri (leather), cover (top), 2–3, 37 (front), Russell Shively, 12 (middle), SebStock, 18 (back), serg_dibrova, 22 (middle), skvoor (state outline), 37 (front), ssuaphotos (open book), 12-13 (back), 42–43 (back), titelio, 21 (top left), 37 (bottom), 43 (bottom), Valentin Agapov (book), 29 (bottom), Vladimir Korostyshevskiy, 20 (bottom back), Volina, 10–11, vovan, 32-33 (back), Walter G. Arce, 38 (left); Wikipedia: Darryl Moran, 19 (bottom), kaatiya, 18 (bottom)

Printed in the United States of America in Stevens Point, Wisconsin.
102011   006404WZS12

TABLE OF CONTENTS

SPORTING SIMILARITIES 4

CHAPTER 1
GETTING THE GOLD 6

CHAPTER 2
WHAT TO WEAR 12

CHAPTER 3
TOOLS OF THE TRADE 20

CHAPTER 4
RULES AND SCORING 26

CHAPTER 5
CHANGING THE FACE OF SPORTS 30

CHAPTER 6
FAMOUS RIVALRIES 34

CHAPTER 7
SPORTS AND POP CULTURE 38

GLOSSARY 46

READ MORE 47

INTERNET SITES 47

INDEX 48

Sporting Similarities

The musics PUMPS.

The crowd erupts in CHEERS.

The competition BLAZES.

There are few things that get crowds more excited than a dynamic sporting event. From ancient to modern times, sports have offered fans plenty of action. In fact, some ancient sports are surprisingly similar to activities enjoyed today. For example, people in ancient Rome raced chariots. Compare this sport to modern auto racing.

Two or four horses pulled the two-wheeled chariots. The chariots raced around the oval track at about 23 miles (37 kilometers) per hour.

Almost 250,000 people could watch races at Circus Maximus. The stadium was built so thousands of fans could view races from the surrounding hills.

Races usually consisted of seven laps around the track for a total of about 3 miles (5 km). Each race lasted eight to nine minutes.

Today drivers use souped-up cars to race around tracks. Like the ancient Roman tracks, many modern tracks are oval. But auto racers reach speeds of more than 200 miles (322 km) per hour.

Auto racers drive hundreds of laps around tracks. At the Talladega Superspeedway in Alabama, stock car racers drive 500 miles (805 km) in one race.

The largest auto-racing stadium in the world is the Indianapolis Motor Speedway in Indiana. It seats 250,000 people.

Technology has certainly changed how people race. But the goal of winning is still the same.

Chapter 1

Getting the Gold

If you're looking for the best athletes, look no further than the Olympic Games. Today countries from around the world send their best athletes to compete in the events. The Games symbolize harmony between people all working to do their very best. But the Olympics didn't start out as a worldwide event.

The very first Olympic Games were held in Olympia, Greece, in 776 BC. Only men who spoke Greek could take part in the Games. Single women could only watch events. Married women weren't even allowed to watch. If caught watching, a married woman could be killed.

an ancient Greek vase showing an Olympic chariot racer

ANCIENT OLYMPIC SPORTS

RUNNING—During footraces competitors ran the length of the stadium once, twice, or several times. The stadium was about 630 feet (192 meters) long.

BOXING—There were no weight classes in this brutal sport. Opponents were chosen randomly, so a heavyweight could face a lightweight. This sport had few rules. A boxer could hit an opponent when he was down.

WRESTLING—The goal of wrestling was to pin the opponent to the ground three times. Moves such as breaking an opponent's fingers were permitted.

PANKRATION—This sport was a combination of boxing and wrestling. The competition was very violent. Attacks like kicking an opponent in the stomach were legal.

PENTATHLON—This was a five-sport event made up of the long jump, discus throw, javelin throw, wrestling, and a footrace.

OLYMPICS REVIVED

The ancient Olympic Games were held as a religious celebration for the god Zeus. But as the rulers of Greece adopted the Christian religion, they outlawed **pagan** events. The Games were stopped in about AD 394.

In 1894 the International Olympic Committee formed. The first modern Olympic Games were held in 1896 in Athens, Greece.

The Olympic rings are a symbol of the modern Games. The five rings stand for major regions of the world: Africa, North and South America, Asia, Europe, and Oceania.

Most athletes at the ancient Olympic Games competed naked. Only chariot racers were allowed to wear clothes.

>>>> [FACT]

pagan—believing in more than one god

OLYMPIC GAMES

The Olympic Games have featured some incredible athletes. Here is just a sample of the many athletes who have made a name for themselves in the Olympics.

CARL LEWIS

Sport: Track and Field

Lewis is known as one of the best track-and-field stars in the world. In 1999 *Sports Illustrated* named Lewis "Olympian of the Century."

Games	Medals
1984 Summer Olympics	4 gold
1988 Summer Olympics	2 gold, 1 silver
1992 Summer Olympics	2 gold
1996 Summer Olympics	1 gold

OLGA KORBUT

Sport: Gymnastics

Olga Korbut is one of the world's best-known gymnasts. She gained international fame at the 1972 Summer Olympics. Her stunning moves impressed the judges, and her winning smile won the hearts of fans. She has been called one of the most important athletes of the 20th century.

Games	Medals
1972 Summer Olympics	3 gold, 1 silver
1976 Summer Olympics	1 gold, 1 silver

SONJA HENIE

Sport: Figure Skating

Norwegian Sonja Henie was just 11 years old when she competed in her first Olympic Games. She used elements of ballet in her skating routines. She was the first skater to use dance elements in her routines.

Games	Medals
1924 Winter Olympics	none; placed eighth
1928 Winter Olympics	1 gold
1932 Winter Olympics	1 gold
1936 Winter Olympics	1 gold

MICHAEL PHELPS

Sport: Swimming

Phelps was 15 years old when he competed in his first Olympics. In 2008 he broke a record for winning the most gold medals in one Olympics.

Games	Medals
2000 Summer Olympics	none; placed fifth in the 200-meter butterfly
2004 Summer Olympics	6 gold, 2 bronze
2008 Summer Olympics	8 gold

OLYMPIC VIOLENCE AND BOYCOTTS

1984 SUMMER GAMES
LOS ANGELES, CALIFORNIA

The Soviet Union and 13 other nations boycott the Games. They refuse to come as payback for the U.S. boycott of the 1980 Summer Games.

1936 SUMMER GAMES
BERLIN, GERMANY

Spain boycotts the Games to take a stand against Adolf Hitler and the German government. Several Jewish athletes also refuse to participate to protest Hitler's treatment of Jews.

1996 SUMMER GAMES
ATLANTA, GEORGIA

The Centennial Olympic Park bombing kills one person and injures 100 others.

1972 SUMMER GAMES
MUNICH, GERMANY

Eleven members of the Israeli Olympic team are taken hostage and murdered by terrorists. The terrorists hoped their actions would make Israel release 200 Arab terrorists held in Israeli prisons.

In the 1904 Olympic Games, U.S. runner Fred Lorz appeared to have won the marathon. He finished with a time of 3 hours and 13 minutes. That time was far faster than his competitors. Just before receiving the gold medal, organizers figured out how he'd done it so fast. Lorz had hitched a ride with a passing car and rode 11 miles (18 km)!

>>>>> | FACT |

The Olympic Games are about international sportsmanship. But sometimes world problems damage the feeling of goodwill. Throughout history political issues have led to some countries boycotting the Games. Acts of violence have resulted in tragedy at other Games.

1980 SUMMER GAMES
MOSCOW, SOVIET UNION

The United States leads a boycott of the Games. It protests the Soviet invasion of Afghanistan. At least 45 countries participate in the boycott.

1964 SUMMER GAMES
TOKYO, JAPAN

South Africa is not allowed in the Games because of its apartheid policy. The country is not allowed to compete again until 1992.

1956 SUMMER GAMES
MELBOURNE, AUSTRALIA

» The Netherlands, Spain, and Switzerland boycott the Games. They protest the Soviet Union's invasion of Hungary.

» China boycotts the Games. Leaders in China and Taiwan had been fighting over rule of China for years. The strained relationship had become so tense that China refuses to come because Taiwan is allowed to compete.

» Egypt, Iraq, and Lebanon also boycott the Games. Israel, France, and Great Britain had ordered air strikes on Egypt to gain control of the Suez Canal. Egypt, Iraq, and Lebanon refuse to compete to protest these attacks.

boycott—to refuse to take part in something as a way of making a protest
apartheid—the practice of keeping people of different races apart

Chapter 2

What to Wear

Fashion has played a key role in what athletes have worn over the years. From flannel shirts to tight shorts, some old-time uniforms look downright silly today.

BASEBALL UNIFORM FIRSTS

1849: The New York Knickerbockers become the first baseball team to wear uniforms. Players wear blue wool pants, white flannel shirts, and straw hats.

a New York team in uniform in 1903

1916: The Cleveland Indians are the first pro team to add numbers to their uniforms.

1960: The Chicago White Sox are the first pro team to add players' last names to uniforms.

Basketball uniforms have evolved over the years. In the early days, professional players wore sleeveless shirts and long, baggy pants. By the 1920s, players wore medium-length shorts. The first jerseys were made of wool.

1920

By the 1930s, fabrics such as polyester and nylon were used for uniforms. Jerseys were made of mesh so they were lighter and cooler.

In the 1970s and 1980s, uniforms reflected fashion. Shorts were tight and short.

1970

2010

Today basketball shorts are longer and looser. Technology plays a role in what players wear too. Uniforms are made from fabrics that wick away sweat.

13

WOMEN'S WEAR

Historically, female athletes wore what society allowed. In the early 1900s, women wore long skirts, blouses, and hats when playing golf or tennis. These outfits were not practical for physical activity.

Over time the styles of women's athletic clothing changed. But it took some courageous women to stand up for more sports-friendly attire.

In 1893 Mrs. Lena Sittig showed off the duplex bicycle skirt she invented. In 1895 *The New York Times* called it "an ideal suit for cycling, to which even the most prudish could not object."

a woman modeling a bicycle skirt in 1895

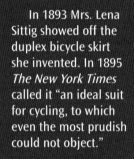

In 1931 tennis player Lili de Alvarez shocked the crowd when she played at Wimbledon. She wore shorts instead of the long dresses that other female players wore. Her shorts weren't like the ones worn today, though. They looked like a skirt divided in the middle.

By 1936 Sonja Henie had set a trend for female figure skaters. She was the first to wear skirts above the knee that allowed her to move freely across the ice. Other skaters of her time wore long, full skirts that didn't allow for much movement.

In 1907 Annette Kellerman was arrested for wearing a one-piece swimsuit. Authorities said the suit showed an indecent amount of her arms and legs. The acceptable swimwear for women at that time was a knee-length dress with tights.

DAZZLING DUDS

Figure skater Katarina Witt dazzled judges with her talent. She earned gold medals in both the 1984 and 1988 Olympic Games.

Witt also dazzled audiences with her outfits. Witt was known for wearing revealing costumes. Her influence can still be seen in figure skating costumes today.

FOOTWEAR

Ancient athletes didn't wear shoes. But bare feet didn't provide the traction needed for speed on the court or field. A lightweight running shoe was first developed in England in the 1900s.

Modern footwear is lighter and more weather resistant than in the past. Scientific research on materials and styles has also much improved what athletes put on their feet.

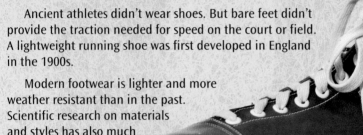

Athletes have worn cleats since at least the 1500s. King Henry VIII is said to have owned a pair. Historians think old-time cleats were made of leather and had leather pieces on the bottom for grip.

Modern-day cleats are made of plastic and vinyl. These materials allow for lighter shoes that grip the ground well. These cleats also don't soak up water like leather cleats did.

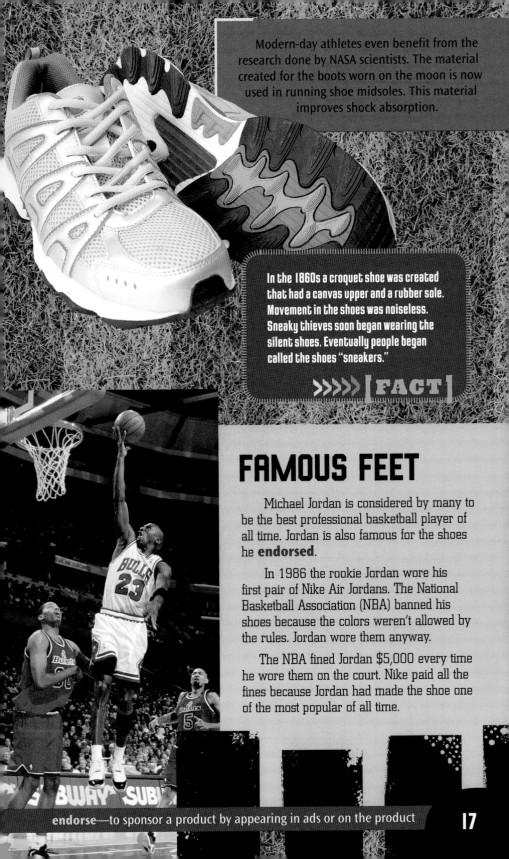

Modern-day athletes even benefit from the research done by NASA scientists. The material created for the boots worn on the moon is now used in running shoe midsoles. This material improves shock absorption.

In the 1860s a croquet shoe was created that had a canvas upper and a rubber sole. Movement in the shoes was noiseless. Sneaky thieves soon began wearing the silent shoes. Eventually people began called the shoes "sneakers."

>>>> [FACT]

FAMOUS FEET

Michael Jordan is considered by many to be the best professional basketball player of all time. Jordan is also famous for the shoes he **endorsed**.

In 1986 the rookie Jordan wore his first pair of Nike Air Jordans. The National Basketball Association (NBA) banned his shoes because the colors weren't allowed by the rules. Jordan wore them anyway.

The NBA fined Jordan $5,000 every time he wore them on the court. Nike paid all the fines because Jordan had made the shoe one of the most popular of all time.

endorse—to sponsor a product by appearing in ads or on the product

SAFETY GEAR

From glass-shattering pucks to crashing cars, sports can be dangerous. Early athletes didn't wear much safety equipment, though.

In the 1800s, hockey players dressed for warmth, not protection. But as the game got rougher, hockey gear needed to provide protection too.

By 1927 women were playing hockey in college. Goalie Elizabeth Graham became the first hockey player to wear a mask when she wore a fencing mask to protect her face.

In 1933 Eddie Shore became the first well-known player to consistently wear a helmet. But the National Hockey League (NHL) didn't officially require helmets until 1979.

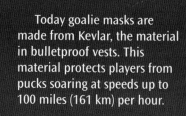

Today goalie masks are made from Kevlar, the material in bulletproof vests. This material protects players from pucks soaring at speeds up to 100 miles (161 km) per hour.

The first football helmets were made of soft leather. These helmets, called head harnesses, helped protect players' ears. But they did nothing to protect the brain. Modern-day helmets are made to help prevent **concussions**. Some helmets have air valves that adjust the helmet to custom-fit players' heads.

In the 1960s, players began wearing pads made of foam and plastic. These materials caused many players to overheat. In 2002 players began wearing pads made from a synthetic fiber created by NASA. This material made pads more breathable and lighter.

DANGEROUS DRIVING

Dale Earnhardt Sr. began racing cars at the age of 15. Earnhardt won 76 major NASCAR races and was named ESPN's ESPY Driver of the Decade for the 1990s. His skill had a big impact on racing. But his death changed racing forever.

It was the last lap of the 2001 Daytona 500. Earnhardt hit the wall in turn four. It hadn't looked like a life-threatening accident to fans. But Earnhardt died in the crash. People everywhere were shocked. Earnhardt's death prompted NASCAR officials to improve safety gear. Racers now:

» race on tracks with SAFER barriers. These crash walls absorb energy to protect drivers.

» have better seat belt systems and roll cages.

» have to wear HANS, a head and neck support system.

concussion—an injury to the brain caused by a hard blow to the head

Chapter 3

Tools of the Trade

The equipment used to play a game is as important as the rules. But that equipment hasn't always looked like it does today. Modern-day balls, racquets, and sticks are made of materials developed with cutting-edge technology. Long ago, sports equipment was made from what people had around them.

Hundreds of years ago, soccer balls were made from pig bladders covered in leather!

Indians played lacrosse long before Europeans arrived in North America. Some tribes used a small, soft ball made of deerskin filled with fur. Others used wood, stone, or baked clay balls. Modern-day lacrosse balls are made of solid rubber.

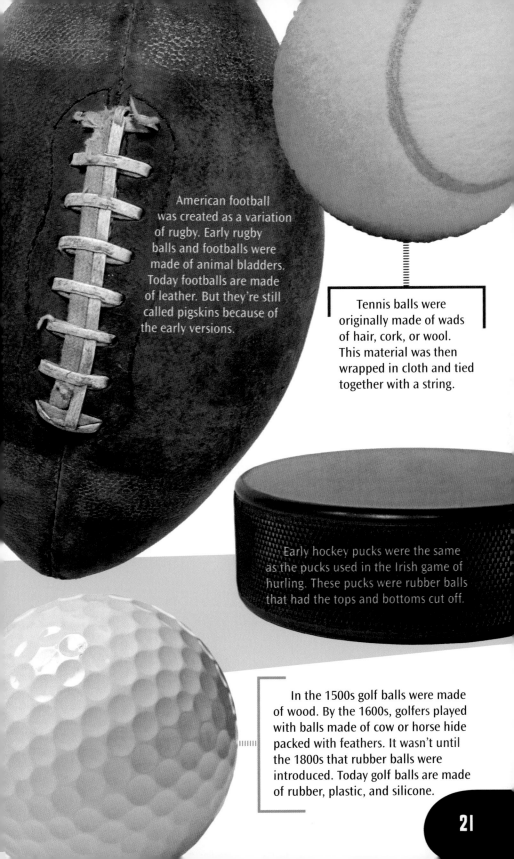

American football was created as a variation of rugby. Early rugby balls and footballs were made of animal bladders. Today footballs are made of leather. But they're still called pigskins because of the early versions.

Tennis balls were originally made of wads of hair, cork, or wool. This material was then wrapped in cloth and tied together with a string.

Early hockey pucks were the same as the pucks used in the Irish game of hurling. These pucks were rubber balls that had the tops and bottoms cut off.

In the 1500s golf balls were made of wood. By the 1600s, golfers played with balls made of cow or horse hide packed with feathers. It wasn't until the 1800s that rubber balls were introduced. Today golf balls are made of rubber, plastic, and silicone.

The first golf clubs were used in Scotland in the 1400s. Early clubs were made of wood. Golf clubs called irons were invented in the 1800s. They were made of heavy metals. Today most club heads are made of titanium, and the **shafts** are made of graphite. These materials are lighter and stronger, allowing players to hit the ball farther or more accurately.

Modern tennis came from a game called jeu de paume. In the early days of the game, players struck the ball with gloved hands. Over time, wooden rackets were invented and used. It wasn't until the 1960s that rackets were crafted out of steel or aluminum.

shaft—the long, narrow section of a club, racket, or bat

IN THE BAG

Tiger Woods has become a legend when it comes to hitting a golf ball. His skill has earned him 71 PGA Tour victories. Here were the clubs in his bag in 2011:

» Driver—Nike VR Tour 8.5

» Irons—Nike VR Pro Blades

» Putter—Nike Method 003

» Wedges—Nike 56 degree VR SW and Nike 60 degree VR LW

» Woods—Nike VR Pro 3 Wood prototype (15 degrees) and Nike SQ II 5 Wood (19 degrees)

Woods' average club head speed is 125 miles (201 km) per hour. The average person's club head speed is 84 miles (135 km) per hour.

>>>>> [FACT]

FAMOUS BASEBALL BATS

Name	Stats	Story
the first Louisville Slugger	length: unknown weight: unknown material: white ash	This bat was made for Pete Browning in 1884. Legend has it that Browning got three hits with the bat in his first game with it. Browning's nickname was the Louisville Slugger, but the name soon came to be used for the bat.
"Black Betsy"	length: 36 inches (91 centimeters) weight: 48 ounces (1.4 kilograms) material: hickory	"Shoeless" Joe Jackson used "Black Betsy" to earn a .356 career batting average. Jackson is considered one of the best hitters in baseball history.
"War Club"	length: unknown weight: 54 ounces (1.5 kg) material: hickory	Babe Ruth reportedly used this massive bat when he started in the major leagues.
world's largest bat	length: 120 feet (37 meters) weight: 68,000 pounds (30,844 kg) material: steel	The world's largest baseball bat sits outside the Louisville Slugger Museum in Louisville, Kentucky.

BRING IN THE MACHINES

Imagine having to wait for someone to set up your bowling pins. Or imagine waiting an hour for workers to resurface the ice for a hockey game. It seems unbelievable now, but early sports players had to do these things. Thanks to modern inventions, players no longer have to wait for the fun to begin.

1 For most of bowling's history, the pins had to be set up by hand. "Pinboys" worked at the ends of bowling lanes to set up the pins.

2 Automated machines that set up pins, called pinspotters, were introduced in 1952.

3 An automatic scoring system that could be used on several lanes at once was patented in 1971.

4 With all the conveniences, today more than 90 million people worldwide bowl for fun.

In the 1800s bowling centers were often gambling centers too. These places had high crime rates. To reduce crime at these centers, Connecticut lawmakers made nine-pin bowling illegal in 1841. To work around the law, players added a tenth pin to the game!

>>>>> [FACT]

The Zamboni drastically reduced wait time at the ice rink. This machine made it quick and easy to remove scratches and chips from the ice.

1942 Frank Zamboni decided to find a better way to clean the ice in his rink in Paramount, California. The machine he created used parts from a Jeep and a fighter plane.

1949 A Zamboni was used on the ice for the first time. It had a 77-inch (196-cm) blade that weighed 57 pounds (25 kg). The blade was dragged behind the machine's back wheels to scrape off a thin layer of ice.

1960 Zambonis were used at the Winter Olympics in Squaw Valley, California.

2008 During the Vancouver Olympic Games, another brand of resurfacing machine was used to clear the ice. The machines leaked water and destroyed the ice. Olympic officials brought in a Zamboni from 600 miles (966 km) away to help clean up the mess.

Chapter 4

Rules and Scoring

In the 1940s, TV broadcasting was a new invention. As a way to spur interest in TV, networks decided to broadcast sporting events. This decision made both TV and sports more popular. But putting sporting events on TV had a big impact on how games were played. TV leaders demanded that sports be faster and more interesting.

The invention of the shot clock in 1954 sped up basketball games for TV viewers and fans in the stands. The rules were changed, stating teams could only keep the ball for a set number of seconds before shooting.

HOME   GUEST

PERIOD 4

BONUS · POSS ·

In 1979 the NBA added the three-point shot. This new way of scoring added excitement to the game.

FOULS SHOT CLOCK FOULS

TV introduced instant replay in 1963. Referees and umpires found themselves under extreme **scrutiny**. Fans could watch a play in slow motion. Viewers could see when referees made the wrong call.

This technology led to many sports using instant replay to review calls. In professional football, coaches can now challenge a set number of calls. Then these plays are reviewed, and sometimes calls are reversed. In tennis, players can also challenge a certain number of calls.

Professional soccer is feeling the pressure to use instant replay—especially since the 2010 World Cup. Fans and reporters cried foul many times during the World Cup games. Many fans argued that England's Frank Lambard had scored against Germany. But the referee said it wasn't a goal. Soccer doesn't allow instant replay, so the call stood.

In most sports whoever scores the most or is the fastest wins. But winning isn't so clear in a sport such as figure skating. In this sport judges use their opinions to score competitors. This form of judging has led to some sticky situations. Some major changes to scoring were adopted after Olympic judges were accused of cheating.

During the 2002 Winter Olympic Games, North American TV viewers were furious. Canadian pairs skaters Jamie Salé and David Pelletier came in second to Russian skaters Elena Berezhnaya and Anton Sikharulidze.

The Russians had made one technical error in their performance. The Canadian pair had skated perfectly. Reports swirled that one of the judges had been pressured to score the Russians higher.

Olympic officials later awarded both the Russian and Canadian pairs gold medals.

The scandal prompted the International Skating Union to make huge changes. The organization spent millions of dollars developing a new scoring system.

The new scoring rules award points based on required moves. Some skaters feel the new rules saved the sport. Others believe the system is too complicated and destroys creativity.

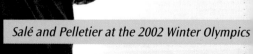

Salé and Pelletier at the 2002 Winter Olympics

When some football players score a touchdown, they do a dance or ham it up for the audience. Long, elaborate celebrations delay the game. In 2009 the NFL changed the rules on touchdown celebrations. Players are allowed to dunk or spike the ball. They can also jump up to the crowd in Lambeau Leaps, and do spins or dances. But any other actions earn the player's team a 15-yard penalty.

NFL RULE BOOK CHANGES

1876 The first rules for American football are written down.

1898 The score for a touchdown changes from four to five points.

1904 The score for a field goal is changed from five to four points.

1909 A field goal drops from four to three points.

1912 Points for a touchdown go up to six points.

1956 For night games, teams begin using a leather ball with white end stripes. This replaces a white ball with black stripes.

1978 The number of regular season games is increased from 14 to 16.

1979 Safety rules are put in place, including no blocking below the waist during kickoffs, punts, and field-goal attempts.

1996 Another safety rule is created. Any hit with the helmet or to the head by a defender is considered a personal foul, and the offending player will be fined.

2009 After a head injury, players must be cleared by team doctors and an outside consultant before returning to the game.

Chapter 5

Changing the Face of Sports

There was a time when most sports stars were white men. That is no longer true. But it took some brave people to challenge the status quo.

American Indian athlete **JIM THORPE** won two Olympic track-and-field gold medals. He went on to have a successful baseball and football career. He is remembered as one of the greatest athletes ever.

1908

1912

1936

African-American track-and-field star **JESSE OWENS** traveled to Berlin, Germany, for the 1936 Summer Olympics. German leader Adolf Hitler expected Germany's white athletes to be superior. But Owens proved him wrong. Owens won four gold medals.

JACK JOHNSON began boxing during a time when blacks and whites were **segregated**. Black people were not allowed to do many things, including box for the heavyweight title. In 1908 reigning heavyweight champ Tommy Burns agreed to fight Johnson. In the 14th round, the fight was finally stopped. Johnson was declared the winner. He became the first African-American to win the title of Heavyweight Champion of the World.

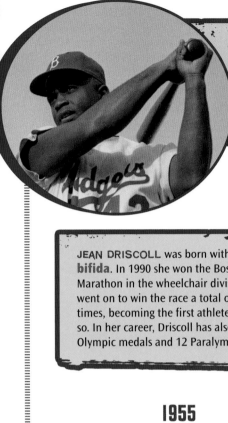

JACKIE ROBINSON became the first African-American to play in major-league baseball. Robinson played for the Brooklyn Dodgers during this history-changing event.

JEAN DRISCOLL was born with **spina bifida**. In 1990 she won the Boston Marathon in the wheelchair division. She went on to win the race a total of eight times, becoming the first athlete to do so. In her career, Driscoll has also won two Olympic medals and 12 Paralympic medals.

1955

1947

1990

ROBERTO CLEMENTE became one of the first Latinos to play in major-league baseball. In 1973 he became the first Latino inducted into the Baseball Hall of Fame.

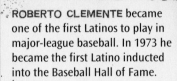

segregate—to keep people of different races apart
spina bifida—a birth defect in which the spinal cord or its coverings don't completely develop

WOMEN IN SPORTS

BABE DIDRIKSON ZAHARIAS

(June 26, 1911–September 27, 1956)

While most people are content to master one sport, Babe Didrikson Zaharias excelled at many. She was an All-American amateur basketball player. She won three track-and-field medals at the 1932 Olympics.

After the Olympics, she was a professional golfer. She won 41 tournaments as a pro. In 1950 the *Associated Press* voted her "Greatest Female Athlete of the first half of the 20th century."

ALTHEA GIBSON

(August 25, 1927–September 28, 2003)

Althea Gibson blazed her way through racial segregation on the tennis courts. She was the first African-American named Female Athlete of the Year by the *Associated Press*. She was also the first African-American to win the French Open, U.S. Open, Australian Doubles, and Wimbledon.

Female athletes have accomplished a lot over the years. Long ago, many people didn't feel it was ladylike for women to compete in sports. It took some determined trailblazers to make people take female athletes seriously.

JACKIE JOYNER-KERSEE

(March 3, 1962–)

Known as one of the greatest female athletes in history, Jackie Joyner-Kersee was a track-and-field star. She won a silver medal in the **heptathlon** at the 1984 Olympic Games. In 1988 she won Olympic gold in both the heptathlon and the long jump. In 1992 she won another Olympic gold medal for the heptathlon and a bronze in the long jump. In 1996 she won a bronze in long jump.

ANNIKA SORENSTAM

(October 9, 1970–)

Born and raised in Sweden, Annika Sorenstam became a pro golfer in 1992. She went on to win 72 Ladies Professional Golf Association (LPGA) tournaments, including 10 major titles. She made history in 2003 when she played in a men's tournament. In 2008 she retired from the game, but she is remembered as the woman with the most golf wins to her name.

heptathlon—a competition made up of 100-meter hurdles, long jump, javelin throw, shot put, 200-meter dash, high jump, and 800-meter run

Chapter 6
Famous Rivalries

>>>>>

Competition is the name of the game in sports. Many people play, but there can only be one winner. That's why **rivalries** begin.

SECRETARIAT VS. SHAM

Secretariat is considered by many to be the best racehorse that ever lived. But some thought a Thoroughbred named Sham could beat Secretariat. A rivalry began. In the 1973 Kentucky Derby and Preakness races, Sham came in second to Secretariat. Then came the Belmont Stakes. Fans believed it would be a close race. But Sham came in last, and Secretariat won by an astonishing 31 **lengths**.

Secretariat

FEDERER VS. NADAL

This may be the greatest tennis rivalry of all time. Switzerland's Roger Federer and Spain's Rafael Nadal were ranked the top two players in the world from 2005 to 2010. No two players have met in Grand Slam finals more than these rivals.

Federer

Nadal

rivalry—a fierce feeling of competition between two people or teams
length—a unit of measure in horse racing; a length is about 8 feet (2.4 m)

ALI VS. FRAZIER

The competition between boxers Muhammad Ali and Joe Frazier has been called the best sports rivalry of all time. They faced off only three times, but their matches were dramatic. In March 1971, they met in Madison Square Garden. Frazier was named the winner. But both were hospitalized for their injuries.

In January 1974 they met again. This time Ali dominated.

Their final match-up took place in 1975. The fight was called the Thrilla in Manila. Both fighters were in good shape. Eventually, Frazier's trainer pulled him from the ring. Ali claimed victory but collapsed in exhaustion after the fight.

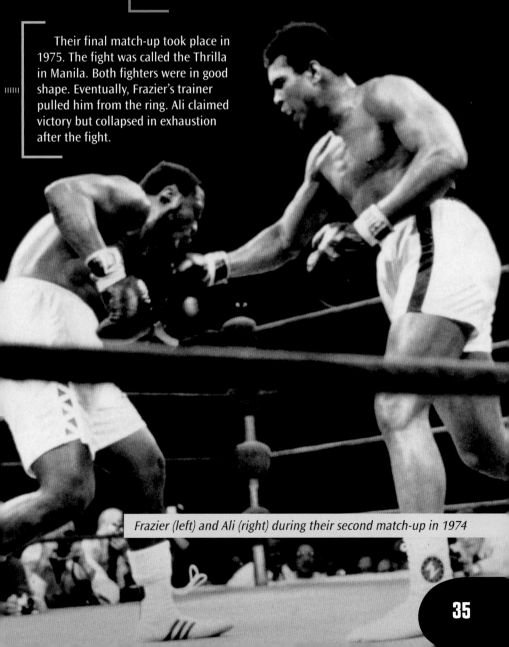

Frazier (left) and Ali (right) during their second match-up in 1974

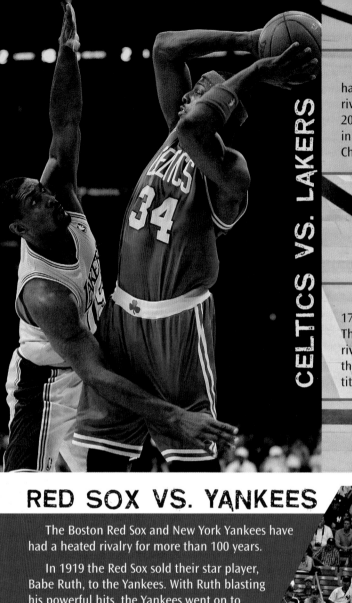

CELTICS VS. LAKERS

The Celtics and Lakers have one of the most famous rivalries in basketball. By 2010 these teams had met in the finals of the NBA Championships 12 times.

By 2011 the Celtics had 17 NBA Championship titles. The Lakers had 16. These rivals hold the records for the first and second most titles in the NBA.

RED SOX VS. YANKEES

The Boston Red Sox and New York Yankees have had a heated rivalry for more than 100 years.

In 1919 the Red Sox sold their star player, Babe Ruth, to the Yankees. With Ruth blasting his powerful hits, the Yankees went on to become the most powerful team in baseball.

The Yankees frustrated the Sox for decades, winning more championships than any other team. The Sox waited more than 80 years after the sale of Ruth to win another World Series. Red Sox fans blamed the losing streak on Ruth and the Yankees. So games between the teams are heated, even today.

ALABAMA VS. AUBURN

One of the fiercest rivalries is between the football team from The University of Alabama and Auburn University. The rivalry began in 1893, and it still divides Alabama today.

The Iron Bowl is the name of the annual game between the teams. For most fans, it's the most important game of the year.

THE UNIVERSITY OF ALABAMA
TUSCALOOSA, AL

AUBURN UNIVERSITY
AUBURN, AL

In 1907 the two university teams had a huge disagreement over some small matters. They argued over where the referees would come from and how much money players would get for food each day. The fight grew so heated, the teams didn't meet again until 1948. When they finally did agree to play again, they couldn't agree to play at either school. So that game—and every other game until 1989—was held in Birmingham, a neutral site.

Chapter 7

Sports and Pop Culture

Athletes can make a great deal of money playing their sports. However, one of the biggest money makers for sports stars comes from endorsements. Many big companies pay athletes to be spokespeople for their products.

Basketball player LeBron James endorses companies such as McDonald's, Coca-Cola, and Nike. Nike signed him with a deal worth $90 million.

Danica Patrick is a popular Indy and NASCAR driver. She's also a popular celebrity endorser. Patrick has done ads for Motorola, Go Daddy, Honda, Secret antiperspirant, and XM Satellite Radio. From June 2006 to June 2007, she made $5 million in endorsements.

TEST YOUR KNOWLEDGE OF SPORTS ENDORSEMENTS

1 | Which famous female athlete has endorsed the sports drink Gatorade?

SOCCER STAR MIA HAMM

BASKETBALL STAR CANDACE PARKER

SNOWBOARDING STAR ELLERY HOLLINGSWORTH

2 | What company has been endorsed by Tiger Woods, Michael Jordan, and Maria Sharapova?

| PUMA | NIKE | ADIDAS |

3 | What golfer made more than $52 million in endorsements in 2010?

ERNIE ELS

MORGAN PRESSEL

PHIL MICKELSON

>>>> FACT

Scientists at the University of Florida created Gatorade for the school's football team. The university's mascot is an alligator, which is how the drink got its name.

ANSWERS: 1. all of them; 2. Nike; 3. Phil Mickelson

BEYOND SPORTS

Famous athletes have celebrity power. Many athletes use their status to support charities and other causes. Some athletes also use their fame and fortune to succeed in other careers.

Former pro wrestler Dwayne "the Rock" Johnson has starred in a number of movies. In 2002 he starred in *The Scorpion King*. He earned $5 million and a place in the Guinness Book of World Records. The record was for

Tennis stars and sisters Venus and Serena Williams are famous on the court and the catwalk. Serena started her clothing line ANERES in 2004. Venus has run her line, called EleVen, since 2007. Venus even wears her line of trendy tennis clothes on the court.

Venus wearing an item from her line EleVen

Football players and brothers Tiki and Ronde Barber used their personal stories to become children's book authors. Their books include *Game Day*, *Red Zone*, and *Go Long!*

PLAYERS IN THE HISTORY BOOKS

BABE RUTH

His real name was George Herman Ruth but he was known as Babe. Babe helped the Boston Red Sox win three World Series titles. After being sold to the New York Yankees, he helped the Yankees win four World Series titles. Yankee stadium became known as the "House that Ruth Built." Babe hit 714 home runs in 22 seasons, a record that wasn't broken until 1974.

At 7 feet, 1 inch (216 cm) tall and 275 pounds (125 kg), Wilt Chamberlain was a dominating basketball figure. It has been nearly 40 years since he retired. But he still holds the records for:

» most games where he scored 50 points or more: 118

» scoring the most in a single game: 100 points

» most career rebounds: 23,924

WILT CHAMBERLAIN

PELÉ

Some say Pelé is the best soccer star ever to play the game.

» His real name is Edson Arantes do Nascimento.

» During his career, he scored 1,281 goals in 1,363 games.

» He holds the world record of 92 **hat tricks**.

hat trick—the scoring of three goals in one game by a single player

JACK NICKLAUS

Known as the Golden Bear, golfer Jack Nicklaus won 73 PGA Tour events. He also won 18 major championships.

MARTINA NAVRATILOVA

Martina Navratilova is considered one of the greatest female tennis players of all time. She won a total of 20 Wimbledon titles. In 2003 she won the Wimbledon mixed doubles title at the age of 46 years, 261 days, becoming the oldest Wimbledon champion.

WAYNE GRETSKY

Known as "The Great One," Wayne Gretsky is considered the best ice hockey player of all time. His jersey number 99 has been retired by all NHL teams.

BO JACKSON

Bo Jackson played both professional football and professional baseball. In fact, he was named to the All-Star team in both sports—the first athlete ever to do so.

REMARKABLE EVENTS IN SPORTS HISTORY

1891

Dr. James Naismith invented the game of basketball. Naismith worked as a physical education teacher for Springfield College in Massachusetts. Naismith had been asked to create an indoor game for the students. He used an outdoor game he played as a child for his inspiration.

1954

British runner Roger Bannister completed a mile in 3 minutes and 59.4 seconds. He became the first person to run a mile in less than 4 minutes.

1976

At just 14 years old, Nadia Comaneci became the first gymnast to score a perfect 10 in an Olympic competition. In fact, she earned seven perfect 10s at the 1976 Summer Games.

1986–1987

Dan Buettner took a team of four Americans on a 15,500-mile (24,945-km) bicycle ride from Prudhoe Bay, Alaska, to Tierra del Fuego, Argentina. The ride set a Guinness World Record in long-distance cycling.

2005
The largest skate park in the world opened in Shanghai, China. It has a skatable area of more than 147,466 square feet (13,700 square meters). That area is equal to 52½ tennis courts!

2007
Martin Strel became the first person to swim the Amazon River, the longest river on Earth.

2007
Pro Indy car driver Logan Gomez beat Alex Lloyd by 0.0005 of a second at the Chicagoland 100. Logan holds a world record for the closest margin of victory in a car race.

2010
John Isner of the United States and Nicolas Mahut of France played the longest tennis match ever. Set at Wimbledon, the match took 11 hours and 5 minutes. Isner finally won with a final score of 70–68 in the fifth set.

Where will sports go from here? No doubt athletes will be faster and stronger and break more records. Sports equipment will continue to evolve to keep up with athletes' needs and demands. No matter the changes, sports fans will always be thrilled by the performances they witness.

GLOSSARY

apartheid (uh-PAR-tayt)—the practice of keeping people of different races apart

boycott (BOY-kot)—to refuse to take part in something as a way of making a protest

concussion (kuhn-KUH-shuhn)—an injury to the brain caused by a hard blow to the head

endorse (in-DORS)—to sponsor a product by appearing in ads or on the product

hat trick (HAT TRIK)—the scoring of three goals in one game by a single hockey or soccer player

heptathlon (hep-TATH-luhn)—a competition made up of 100-meter hurdles, long jump, javelin throw, shot put, 200-meter dash, high jump, and 800-meter run

length (LENGKTH)—a unit of measure in horse racing; a length is about 8 feet (2.4 m)

pagan (PAY-guhn)—believing in more than one god

rivalry (RYE-val-ree)—a fierce feeling of competition between two people or teams

scrutiny (SKROO-tuh-nee)—close examination

segregate (SEG-ruh-gate)—to keep people of different races apart in schools and other public places

shaft (SHAFT)—the long, narrow section of a club, racket, or bat

spina bifida (SPIN-uh BIF-i-duh)—a birth defect in which the two sides of the spine don't completely enclose the spinal cord

READ MORE

Bailey, Diane. *Great Moments in World Cup History.* World Soccer Books. New York: Rosen Central, 2010.

Berman, Len. *The Greatest Moments in Sports.* Naperville, Ill.: Sourcebooks, 2009.

Mason, Paul. *Sports Heroes of Ancient Greece.* Crabtree Connections. New York: Crabtree Pub. Co., 2011.

Raum, Elizabeth. *Famous Athletes.* Chicago: Raintree, 2008.

Stout, Glenn. *Yes She Can!: Women's Sports Pioneers.* Good Sports. Boston: Houghton Mifflin Harcourt, 2011.

INTERNET SITES

FactHound offers a safe, fun way to find Internet sites related to this book. All of the sites on FactHound have been researched by our staff.

Here's all you do:

Visit *www.facthound.com*

Type in this code: 9781429675376

INDEX

Ali, Muhammad, 35
auto racing, 4, 5, 19, 38, 45

baseball, 12, 23, 30, 31, 36, 42, 43
basketball, 13, 17, 26, 32, 36, 38,
    39, 42, 44
bicycling, 14, 44
bowling, 24
boxing, 6, 30, 35

Chamberlin, Wilt, 42
chariot racing, 4, 5, 6, 7
Clemente, Roberto, 31
clothing, 7, 12–13, 14–15

Didrikson Zaharias, Babe, 32
Driscoll, Jean, 31

Earnhardt Sr., Dale, 19
endorsements, 17, 38–39

Federer, Roger, 34
figure skating, 9, 15, 28
football, 19, 21, 27, 29, 30, 37,
    41, 43
Frazier, Joe, 35

Gibson, Althea, 32
golf, 14, 21, 22, 23, 32, 33, 39, 43
Gretsky, Wayne, 43
gymnastics, 8, 44

Henie, Sonja, 9, 15
hockey, 18, 21, 24, 43

instant replay, 27

Jackson, Bo, 43
Jackson, "Shoeless" Joe, 23
James, LeBron, 38
Johnson, Jack, 30

Jordan, Michael, 17, 39
Joyner-Kersee, Jackie, 33

Korbut, Olga, 8

Lewis, Carl, 8

Nadal, Rafael, 34
Navratilova, Martina, 43
Nicklaus, Jack, 43

Olympics
    ancient, 6, 7
    modern, 6, 7, 8–9, 10–11, 15,
        25, 28, 30, 31, 32, 33, 44
Owens, Jesse, 30

Patrick, Danica, 38
Pelé, 42
Phelps, Michael, 9

rivalries, 34–37
Robinson, Jackie, 31
Ruth, Babe, 23, 36, 42

safety, 18–19, 29
Secretariat, 34
Sham, 34
shoes, 16–17, 39
soccer, 20, 27, 39, 42
Sorenstam, Annika, 33
sports equipment, 20–25
swimming, 9, 15, 45

tennis, 14, 21, 22, 27, 32, 34, 41,
    43, 45
Thorpe, Jim, 30
track and field, 6, 8, 30, 32, 33, 44
TV, affects on rules, 26–27

Witt, Katarina, 15
Woods, Tiger, 23, 39